THE
MOSAIC
SOURCEBOOK

THE
MOSAIC
SOURCEBOOK

Paul Siggins & Paul Cooper

■

Text by Jenna Jarman

Photography by Richard Foster

Trafalgar Square Publishing

For Fiona, Phoebe, Jess, and Carol.
Thanks for the support.

First published in the
United States of America in 1997 by
Trafalgar Square Publishing
North Pomfret, Vermont 05053
Reprinted in 1998

Printed in Hong Kong

Editorial Director:	Suzannah Gough
Senior Editor:	Jenna Jarman
Editorial Assistant:	Helen Woodhall
Designer:	Amanda Lerwill
Stylist:	Tiffany Davis
Art Direction:	Sue Storey assisted by Amanda Lerwill
Illustrations	Chris and Elly King
Production:	Mano Mylvaganam

Library of Congress Catalog Card Number: 97-60188

ISBN 1-57076-098-5

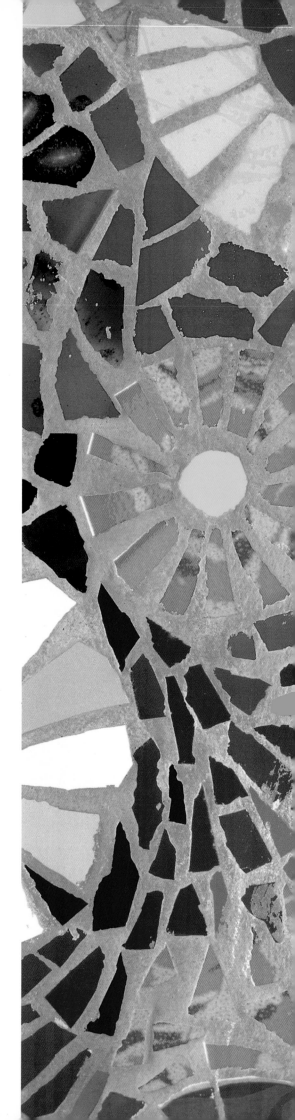

CONTENTS

Foreword

As contemporary mosaicists who like to have freedom with design, we take our inspiration from a wide range of sources, from classical mosaic art to contemporary culture. Our approach is characteristically simple and understated, but we enjoy working in a variety of styles and often incorporate bold colors and motifs into our designs.

Our view on materials is that there should be as few restrictions as possible — if it doesn't perish then you can mosaic with it. In addition to traditional tesserae, we also use glass beads, buttons, pebbles, and shells among other things, and have a large collection of ceramic tiles, gathered from years of rummaging around flea markets, garage and yard sales, and tile suppliers' discontinued shelves. With these materials we produce all sorts of mosaic pieces — decorative objects, wall hangings, floor panels, as well as more unusual three-dimensional forms, such as mannequins, busts, and clocks.

Although mosaic is a relatively simple and certainly accessible craft, it can seem daunting to the uninitiated. In this book, we aim to give all the information a beginner needs to get started, and also to provide the more experienced with a rich source of innovative designs and motifs. For us, mosaic is a highly rewarding and therapeutic craft, and we hope that everyone will share in our enjoyment of it, both as an art form and as an outlet for self-expression.

Introduction

The ancient art of mosaic is enjoying a new and exciting surge of popularity, both as a craft and as a consumer item. No longer is mosaic associated only with classical and religious works of art, or the gaudier designs of the Seventies. Today, mosaic is a highly flexible medium at the cutting edge of design, and there are striking mosaic borders, panels, and murals decorating homes, restaurants, bars, and offices everywhere. Capable of taking on many guises, mosaic can be simply defined as a pattern or image consisting of small pieces of material, called tesserae, which covers a surface. The possibilities are endless in terms of designs, materials, and uses – for both decorative objects and architectural features – and more and more people are realizing how rewarding yet accessible mosaic is as a craft or hobby.

Mosaic was hugely popular during classical antiquity and the Middle Ages, and both periods produced many great works of art. It was, however, reserved only for those wealthy enough to commission what was a very expensive medium – during the Middle Ages, for example, mosaic was almost exclusively the preserve of the Church. Its role was to some extent a subservient one to that of painting – Roman and Hellenistic works were created chiefly as durable copies of paintings and frescoes, and medieval mosaicists, although appreciating mosaic's special luminous qualities, strove to bring their art as close to painting as possible. This confusion between the two disciplines helped lead to the decline of mosaic during the

The sea was the source of inspiration for the design of this mirror frame, decorated in complementary shades of blue vitreous glass tesserae. It was an experimental piece made while we were developing our two-dimensional relief frames.

Renaissance, and it is only relatively recently that mosaic has been reevaluated, and that the means of production have brought mosaic within the reach of ordinary people.

In the 19th century, attitudes toward mosaic began to change. Not only was it beginning to be put on an industrial and commercial basis, but certain artists were also questioning its role and revitalizing it as an art form. The innovative use of materials by Catalan artist and architect Antonio Gaudí (1852–1926), for example, was key in modernizing mosaic style. By mixing materials and techniques in contemporary, nonrepresentational designs, Gaudí was particularly influential – his wild and wonderful, largely exterior mosaics made up of smalti, broken glass, china, and ceramic, showed how large surfaces could be decorated with inexpensive, alternative materials. Form and style were revitalized and the way was now open for mosaic to expand.

In the mid-20th century, the mass production of vitreous glass tesserae brought material costs down and so broadened the appeal of mosaic. This significant step forward had its disadvantages, however, since it led to a plethora of uninspired mosaics from the Fifties onward – a trend which reached its nadir in the Seventies when, for many, mosaic was synonymous with the decoration of swimming pools. Fortunately, individual artists continued to make innovative and interesting mosaics during this period and now mainstream mosaic is not only within everyone's reach, but it is also recognized as an exciting and stylish medium in its own right.

You can use an endless variety of materials to create mosaics. For this one, we used glass beads, broken ceramics, cut tesserae, and a reclaimed art deco border on a base of medium-density fiberboard. The wrought-iron frame was specially created but you could use a ready-made one.

to catch the light, for example, and the interstices or spacing between tesserae can be widened to maximize stylization, or else tightly packed for a more painterly effect. Making mosaics is not only easy but can also be immensely satisfying and therapeutic – as with a jigsaw or collage, this craft has an almost childlike appeal because the tesserae are carefully pieced together to form a whole. Perhaps the most appealing thing about mosaic, however, is the huge flexibility it offers, in terms of individual choices of materials and textures, as well as designs, styles, and uses. Mosaics can be made to fit any style or interior whether traditional or contemporary. Most of the projects in this book are particularly well suited to contemporary interiors, but they still incorporate classical and traditional designs, and with the broad mix of color schemes and motifs on hand, there are styles to suit all tastes.

Everything depends on the mix of colors and materials and, as this book demonstrates, a mosaic can be as vibrantly

Although capable of producing stunning results, mosaic does not necessarily demand artistic flair, nor even good drawing skills. The stylized quality of mosaic means that even the simplest designs can be strikingly effective. There is a wealth of source material available both in this book and elsewhere – from classic to contemporary designs – for you to refer to or copy. And the original design is just the beginning – tesserae can be set at varying angles

ABOVE LEFT: *This table is made of carved plywood, and the snake is made from cement resin. The tesserae are all one color so that the snake blends in with the rest of the mosaic, as it does with its environment in nature.*
ABOVE: *The use of smalti gives this asp vessel a timeless appearance – the aim was to create the kind of mosaic which could have adorned an ancient temple, perhaps concealing mysterious and dark secrets.*

good starting point for the beginner. And since mosaic covers a multitude of sins, such as dull colors or hideous patterns, even old or ugly items can be transformed completely. But tackling larger surfaces or objects doesn't have to be daunting, although this will obviously take longer; time can be saved if smaller mosaic pieces or panels are mixed in with plain areas (see pages 22–23.) And because very little in the way of specialist tools and equipment is needed, anybody can start making mosaics with a minimum investment. So, whatever your needs and whatever your style, mosaic has something to offer you. This book will get beginners started on this fascinating craft and will inspire the more experienced, enabling everyone to produce stunning mosaics for friends and for the home.

patterned or as subtle and understated as needed. The possibilities for both colors and materials are endless – commercially produced tesserae offer an infinite spectrum of colors and an interesting range of textures, from shiny glass to smooth porcelain, glossy or matte ceramic. The grouting can be any color you wish. Then there are the more unusual materials to consider, such as pebbles, shells, and beads, to name just a few.

But the choices don't end there – mosaic can be used not only to cover floors and walls, but also to decorate furniture and other objects around the home. Small or portable objects are obviously a

ABOVE: *On one side of this urn, blazing reds and golds reflect the vibrancy of the sun; on the other, softer colors depict the moon.*

ABOVE RIGHT: *The extravagant use of silver-leaf mosaic on this large mirror frame is complemented by the simplicity of the scrolled form. To keep costs down, silver leaf can be combined with other materials, such as porcelain tesserae, as in the silver star picture frame project on page 38.*

How to use this book

The following notes explain what each section of the book is about and how it should be used, either by the complete beginner or the more experienced craftsperson.

TECHNIQUES, TOOLS, AND MATERIALS

Techniques (pages 14–23) Despite potentially stunning results, the technique for mosaic is surprisingly simple. It is easily explained and easy to learn, and has hardly changed since ancient times. It involves cutting materials into basic shapes, pasting them into place according to a pattern, and then setting the mosaic with grout. In this section, the two techniques – the direct and indirect methods – are both clearly explained with comprehensive step-by-step photography for two easy projects. The key differences between the two methods, and their advantages and disadvantages, are outlined so that you can feel confident about deciding which method to use. All of the projects in the book are based on one of these two techniques, to which you can always refer if necessary.

Tools and materials (pages 16–19). A comprehensive list of basic equipment and accompanying photographs is given (see pages 16–17), with items described in detail. Few specialist tools are needed for mosaic – the tile-cutter and nipper (a tool for cutting fairly precise and small shapes) are the only essential ones, and both are inexpensive and easy

to find. Other tools, such as sponges and squeegees, are found in most homes. The possibilities for materials are endless, from commercially available tesserae and tiles (vitreous glass, smalti, and ceramic), to everyday materials (pebbles, broken china, beads, and shells). This section describes the options, providing information on potential uses, availability, cost, advantages, and disadvantages.

PROJECTS

The eight step-by-step projects can all be made within the space of a weekend, and all by the beginner. Some are better suited than others to the complete novice, and this is indicated in each introduction. The look is clean and contemporary throughout, and the projects provide an exciting range of innovative styles and colorways – from a vibrant African-style tabletop to a classically inspired and understated lampbase. With these, you will be able to create all the most popular mosaic pieces that command such high prices in today's best furnishing stores, including picture and mirror frames, garden urns, vases, and decorative dishes – mosaics both for outdoors and for a range of interiors.

The projects use an interesting variety of materials, and color codes are provided for storebought tesserae so that you can reproduce the projects exactly if you wish. Templates and alternative designs for the projects are also provided (see Alternative Designs, right).

This 20-foot-long panel was commissioned for the perfume and cosmetics department of a large store in London, England. The porcelain tesserae of the bottle shapes are cut through with ribbons of gold and silver which seem to move as they catch the light.

ALTERNATIVE DESIGNS

For each project, two alternative designs are provided, using different color schemes, sometimes in a similar style and sometimes giving a completely different look. The kitsch floral vase project, for example, comes with two distinctive alternative designs – one combining pieces of smashed blue-and-white crockery with pale shells to create an unusually delicate effect, the other a lively and abstract pattern incorporating a random mix of red and purple beads. Any of these designs could be adapted to your own color schemes, or applied to other objects, and would work particularly well on similarly shaped ones such as lampbases, and pots of any kind. Once again, the idea is to provide maximum choice and flexibility, while the basic technique illustrated in the step-by-step photography can still be followed. Although still suitable for the beginner – though the complete novice may be advised to try one of the step-by-step projects before experimenting with alternatives – these sixteen alternative designs provide enough original source material to inspire even the most accomplished mosaicist.

TEMPLATES AND MOTIFS

Project templates (pages 78–85). Each project is accompanied by a black-and-white template so that the design can be clearly seen and easily followed. These can be photocopied, enlarged and transferred onto your surface, copied freehand, or used simply as a guideline. You can choose the extent to which you stick to the design – the templates are not obligatory but are simply there for those who feel they need or want them. You could easily adapt the design, change the color scheme, or use the basic template for whatever object you choose (a template for a tabletop, for example, could just as well be used for a dish or plate). None of the designs are overly complicated, though some are obviously simpler than others.

Miscellaneous motifs (pages 86–95). This ten-page section of motifs provides further source material for those looking for new ideas and inspiration. The motifs can be used in a variety of ways: a single motif could be used on a plain background, it could be incorporated into one of the designs provided in the book, or multiple motifs could be dotted randomly over a plain surface or placed deliberately to form a border or central pattern. The possibilities are endless, and, as with the design templates in the book they can be photocopied, traced, or copied freehand. The motifs are shaded so that you can get the right effect using the color scheme of your choice, and the basic methods used are the same as those outlined in the techniques section.

Organized into different categories, the motifs range from the pictorial (flowers, fish, amphibians, shells) to the abstract or geometric (for allover patterns or borders) and offer classical, ethnic, Celtic, art deco, and contemporary styles.

TECHNIQUES

Tools & materials

Most of the following tools and materials are available from mosaic or craft suppliers, and even hardware stores. For information on suppliers, including mail order, see page 96.

TESSERAE

These are the small pieces of material that are built up onto a surface to form mosaic. Those listed below are the most common types, but there are many more to choose from – beads, bottletops, gemstones, scraps of metal (but be careful of rust), as well as stones and pebbles for outdoor mosaics.

Ceramic tiles Household kitchen or bathroom tiles may be plain white, highly colored and patterned, in matte or glossy finishes. They can be an inexpensive option – look out for old or reject tiles, as even the gaudiest ones have potential once they are cut up into small pieces. Smashed dishware is also suitable for mosaic, as are home-fired and painted ceramics. Ceramic is easy enough to cut with a tile-cutter, although maybe not as easy as vitreous glass. It is not usually frost-proof and so not suitable for outdoor mosaics.

Porcelain and vitrified clay These are hard-wearing materials, and so particularly suitable for floors, which can be used for both indoor and outdoor mosaics. Both come in a matte, natural, and muted color range, and will stain easily if not properly sealed. Porcelain is less expensive than vitreous glass and is sold by the sheet (size and number of tesserae vary). Vitrified clay tends to be thicker and therefore slightly more hard-wearing and expensive, as well as more difficult to cut. It is sold either as tiles or tesserae.

Smalti These are thick, rectangular chunks of opaque glass – about ⅜ x ½ x ¼ inch, which are uneven and so suitable whenever a totally flat surface is not required. They come in a vast range of colors, and are glossy and highly reflective – ideal if you want your mosaic to glint and catch the light. Handmade, mainly in Italy, smalti are expensive. They are sold by the pound and all colors are the same price (with the exception of gold and silver). They are suitable for both indoor and outdoor use but not for heavy-duty flooring.

Vitreous glass tesserae These are also made of opaque glass but are thinner and less expensive than smalti. They are manufactured in regular ¾ x ¾ x 1½ inch squares, with a smooth front and rippled back to aid adhesion. They come

in a wide range of colors, although not as wide as that of smalti, and prices vary according to the color. Gold and silver tesserae are the most costly and so best for limited use or highlights. Their thinness and regular shape makes them easy to cut and use, and so they are perfect for the beginner, and can be used when a totally flat surface is required. They are resistant to poor weather conditions and are suitable for outdoor use. Vitreous glass tesserae are sold loose, in single colors, or in mixed bags (usually sold by the pound) or by the sheet (225 tesserae) either in one color only, or ready mixed into a multicolor, simple geometric design. These tesserae are stuck down on paper which you simply peel off, and they can be applied without any nipping or cutting if you want to mosaic a surface quickly.

A number of brands are available, and any can be used for mosaic. For the projects in this book we used Vetricolor (also known as Vitmos). Color codes for this brand are provided so you can reproduce our colors if you wish.

TOOLS

Combed scraper or spreader Used to give an even and grooved bed of adhesive on flat surfaces.

Glass cutter This simple tool has a tungsten wheel to score straight or curved lines on ceramic, vitreous glass, or mirror. Spray the wheel with light lubricating oil before using to make its action smoother.

Hammer and hardie These are traditional tools which are sometimes used for cutting marble and smalti. They require practice and so are not used in this book; the tools described here are more suitable for beginners.

Nippers These are mosaic-cutters or tile-nippers with tungsten tips used for halving or quartering tesserae, or for "nibbling" them into precise shapes. They are ideal when working with vitreous glass tesserae, ceramic tesserae, or smalti, but can be hard work on porcelain or vitrified clay.

Permanent pen For marking designs or guidelines on the surface of objects – water-soluble ink would be rubbed off by adhesive. Do not use on tesserae.

Serrated trowel Used in the same way as a combed scraper but for larger areas, such as walls and floors.

Small pointing trowel Useful for applying adhesive to small, awkward areas.

Squeegees and grout floats These are used for spreading the grout into the joints between tesserae. When using the squeegee, use the blade to drag the grout across; with the grout float, use the edge and not the flat surface.

Straight scraper General adhesive application tool.

Tile cutter and breaker This dual-purpose tool, which comes in either plastic or metal, can both score and cut. The plastic variety has a short life but is inexpensive, and suitable for vitreous glass, ceramic, and thin porcelain. A metal one will last longer and can be used to break harder materials, such as thick porcelain and vitrified clay tiles, as well as ceramic and glass. With both, the scored line is placed in the center of the breaker's jaws which, once shut, will break the tile along the line.

Water-soluble pen For marking guidelines on glazed tesserae for cutting. Note that you should never use this or any pen on unglazed tesserae.

GLUES AND ADHESIVES

Cement This is cheap and strong. It can be used on walls and is ideal for laying external mosaic flooring as long as conditions are frost-free.

Cement-based tiling adhesives These powder-mix adhesives provide long-lasting results (but check the label of different brands for drying times, as these vary) and are suitable for most tesserae and all surfaces that need to be hardwearing, for indoor and outdoor use. When applying to a flexible surface such as wood or board, mix in a flexible additive which will soften the adhesive in case there is any movement in the wood. Quick-setting powder adhesives (a few hours) are also available.

Grout This is a cement mortar which is most often used for setting the finished mosaic. The projects in this book in which there are wide gaps between tesserae use a wide-joint grout (which has a sandy texture). If the interstices are small and tesserae are tightly packed together then grouting is not necessary. It depends on taste – some people prefer the

grouted look, some the ungrouted, though grouting strengthens the mosaic and gives a smoother, less jagged finish. Grouts are available in a range of colors, the basic ones being white, gray, ivory, charcoal, sandstone, and brown. Specialist colored grouts are also available but it is very easy to color them yourself by mixing white grout with acrylic or powder paint (water-based only). Remember that colored grouts will be a couple of shades lighter when dry.

Adhesive sealant Sealant is mixed 1 part to 4 parts water and used to seal all sides of untreated wood to prevent swelling when moisture gets in either during or after the mosaic process. It is also used to seal unglazed ceramic and other porous surfaces. Some people use undiluted household glue both as a sealant and as an adhesive for sticking down tesserae, but this is not recommended as it is not sufficiently durable. Sealant is available from hardware stores and craft suppliers.

Ready-mix tile adhesives These are not as hard-wearing as the powder-mix variety but are convenient and can be bought in smaller quantities. They are hard-wearing enough for indoor decorative glass, ceramic, or wooden objects, but are not recommended for floors. Water-resistant brands are also available and are advisable for mosaics that may get wet or for those on wooden objects, but even non-water-resistant brands are regularly used for bathroom tiling. Combination adhesive-and-grout products are not recommended.

Silicone sealants and multipurpose gap-filling adhesives Both of these are useful for very small tesserae that need to dry quickly, but are not suitable for large areas. They come in tubes or cartridges that fit into a gun which can be used to lay a neat, accurate bead of adhesive along a line. Silicone sealant is slightly more difficult to clean away when dry. These adhesives can be used for glass, plastic, ceramic, metal, and wood.

Washable household glue Mixed 1 part to 3 parts water, glue used to apply tesserae to brown paper for the indirect method. Available from art and craft stores.

SAFETY NOTE Goggles must be worn when cutting tesserae as small bits of material can fly through the air. A mask must be worn when sawing fiberboard, polishing dry grout, and using solvents. Rubber gloves are a must for all procedures involving cement, grout, and acid.

THE DIRECT METHOD

Basic Equipment
Dust mask
Lint-free cloth
Nippers
Pencil
Pots for mixing grout/glue/adhesive
Goggles
Ruler
Scraper
Sponge
Squeegee

Tools
Craft knife
1-inch artist's brush

Materials
Circular block of fiberboard, ¾-inch
  thick and 9 inches in diameter
Sealer (1 part household glue to
  4 parts water)
1 quart pot ready-mixed water-
  resistant tile adhesive
Vitreous glass tesserae (Vetricolor):
  70 x dark blue (20.46.2)
  25 x light blue (20.87.1)
  40 x white (20.10.1)
3-pound bag white wide-joint grout

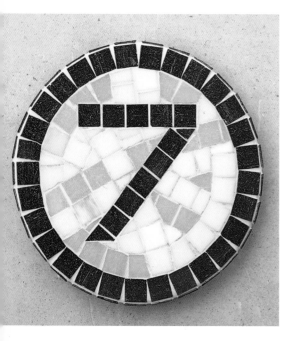

This is a very straightforward method of applying mosaic, in which tesserae are stuck directly onto the chosen object. It is used where the surface does not need to be smooth or completely flat. It is also useful where a large number of colors is being used since the colors of the tesserae remain visible, whereas in the indirect method – where tesserae are stuck face down – only the backs of the tesserae are seen and these are often not colored. This method is also used for 3-D work. It is not so suitable for intricate designs, however, as the adhesive applied to the surface of the object will cover, and at least partly obscure, the design you are following.

A variety of tesserae can be used and combined, including vitreous glass, smalti, mirror, and smashed or broken china, as well as more unusual materials such as pebbles, stones, and beads. The tesserae can be of varying thicknesses and can be deliberately set at different angles to catch the light.

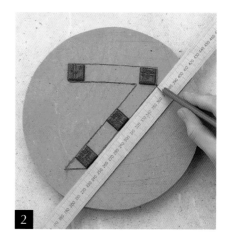

1 If you are working on a wooden or board surface as here, score all over using the craft knife and then prime with sealant, using the artist's brush. Leave to dry.

2 Draw your design on the surface, either freehand, if you feel confident enough, or using a template, basing it on the size of your tesserae. It is also possible to trace designs or use a photocopy of a design.

3 Paste on the adhesive in sections to keep it from drying out and stick down the tesserae (smooth side upward), according to the design. In general we advise leaving a ¹⁄₁₆-inch

grout gap between tesserae, but this depends on the individual project and on personal preference. Here, whole tesserae are stuck down first and the smaller pieces are cut (see Step 4) and stuck down as and when necessary. For projects requiring lots of quarter- or half-tesserae, cut all of them first before starting to paste.

4 To nip the tesserae into smaller pieces – whether wedge-shapes, quarters, or triangles – hold the nippers on the very edge of the tessera as shown, and cut. The whole tessera will then split in a straight line from the point where the nippers are held.

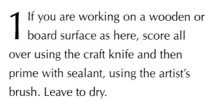

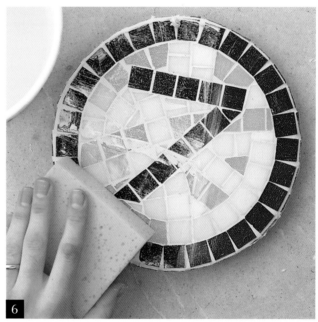

5 Once all the tesserae are stuck down, leave to dry for 24 hours. You will then need to seal the surface of the mosaic by grouting. Gradually mix the grout with water to get the consistency of a thick, creamy paste. Cover the mosaic, including the edge, with a generous amount of grout, using a squeegee or a grout float (or a smaller tool, if necessary, for 3-D work) to ensure that all the gaps and cracks are filled.

6 Wipe off excess grout with the squeegee, and then clean off the residue with a damp sponge. Once the grout has dried – after approximately 24 hours – polish the mosaic with a clean, dry cloth.

THE INDIRECT METHOD

Basic Equipment (see page 20)

Tools
Permanent marker
Water-soluble pen
Tile cutter and breaker (see page 19)
Kitchen towel
Hammer
1-inch artist's brush
Combed scraper/spatula
Block of wood or grout float
Craft knife

Materials
Brown paper
Ceramic tiles 6 inches x 6 inches:
  1 x yellow
  1 x blue
  1 x red
Washable household glue
1 quart ready-mixed
  tile adhesive
3-pound bag white wide-
  joint grout

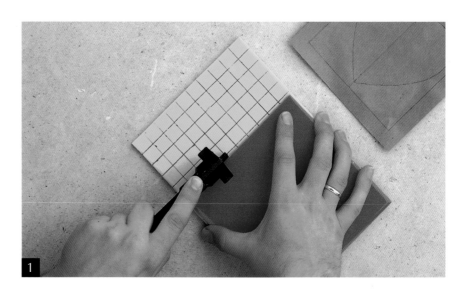

This method is used when a very flat, smooth surface is needed, and involves first sticking tesserae face down onto brown paper. It is ideal for intricate designs which, in the direct method, would be obscured by adhesive. Here the tesserae are stuck onto paper with transparent, washable household glue before the whole mosaic is transferred to your chosen object with adhesive.

It is also the best method for large pieces created off-site, as the design can be drawn on paper and cut into segments, before the whole project is transferred to the site and reassembled like a puzzle. Other reasons for using this method include: working with multiple pieces (it is easier to create several at a time on paper, rather than one at a time with the direct method); working on a horizontal rather than a vertical surface; stopping and starting work on a project (washable household glue can be pasted and then pasted again at a later date, whereas in the direct method, the adhesive will harden quickly and will have to be scraped off, then reapplied).

One of the disadvantages of this method is that when using ceramic tiles, the backs of which are very

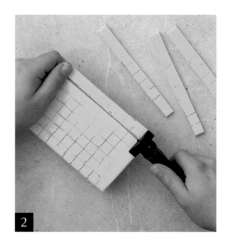

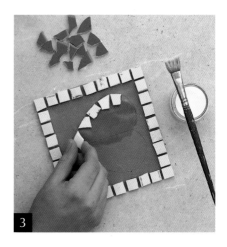

similar, it is difficult to keep track of the colors being used unless you apply the tesserae in a logical order.

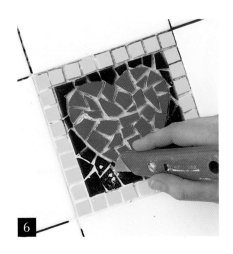

1 Use a permanent marker to draw or trace your design onto brown paper. Next, cut the yellow tile into small squares. To do this, first mark out a grid on the tile, using water-soluble ink and a ruler. Here the tile is divided into ⅝-inch squares. Score along all the marked lines with a tile cutter and breaker, pressing it against another tile to give you a straight line.

2 Use the tile cutter and breaker to cut along the score lines as shown, holding it as close against the tile as it will go and lining up the pointer with the scored line. As you cut into the edge, the tile will break along the

entire line. First cut the tile into strips, and then cut the strips into squares. To get irregular-sized pieces (as with the red and blue ones here) either use nippers or wrap the tiles, one at a time, into a kitchen towel and smash them lightly with a hammer – be careful not to smash them to smithereens!

3 Working on one section at a time, apply washable household glue to the brown paper and then stick down the tesserae, making sure that they are face downward. This means that the wrong sides, often all the same color, are face upward. Confusion can be avoided, however, by sticking the tesserae down in the right order. Leave to dry for approximately 12 hours.

4 Apply adhesive to your surface, in this case a wall, using a combed spatula or scraper to give even coverage of approximately ⅛ inch. Lay the paper-backed sheet of mosaic face downward onto the adhesive-covered area, aligning the edges correctly. Push down firmly, using a block of wood or groat float to ensure that the mosaic beds into the adhesive securely. Leave to dry for approximately 24 hours.

5 Dampen the brown paper, using warm water to break down the washable household glue. Once damp, carefully peel the paper off the mosaic in one piece. If there is any resistance, dampen the paper further.

6 Rub the surface of the mosaic vigorously with a wet cloth to remove excess adhesive. If necessary, rake out stubborn areas of adhesive with a craft knife or other suitable tool. Finally, grout, clean, and polish (see Steps 5 and 6, page 21).

PROJECTS

Geometric mirror frame

THIS GEOMETRIC-STYLE BATHROOM MIRROR decorated in vitreous glass tesserae is very simple to make, and so is suitable for complete beginners. There is little nipping required, as most of the tesserae are laid down whole, with only the tesserae used for the borders and edges cut in half, or quartered. It is also inexpensive because the frame can be made cheaply from ¾-inch-thick medium-density fiberboard. We cut the frame ourselves for this project, but if you don't have the right equipment at home, most carpenters or hardware stores should be able to do it for you. Making the frame from fiberboard gives you the advantage of being able to choose the exact size and shape that you want, which will be useful if you have a particular setting in mind. Remember that it is very simple to adjust either the design or spacing of the tesserae to fit your mosaic to an existing frame. An old or ugly frame would do perfectly well here, provided the basic shape is suitable, since it will be completely covered in mosaic.

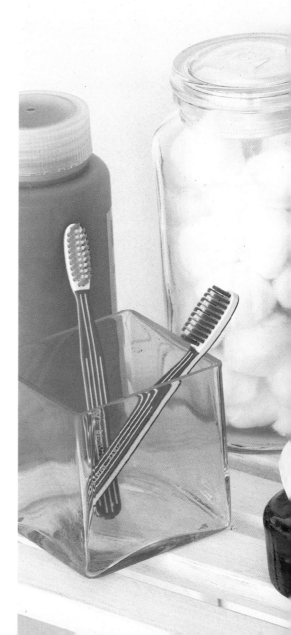

YOU WILL NEED

Basic Equipment (see page 20)

Tools
1-inch artist's brush

Materials
Frame with border 3 inches wide
Mirror
Sealant (1 part household glue to 4
  parts water)
1 quart ready-mixed water-resistant
  tile adhesive
Vitreous glass tesserae (Vetricolor):
  100 x green (20.58.2)
  100 x aqua (20.42.2)
  100 x gray (20.33.1)
  100 x white (20.10.1)
1-pound bag ivory wide-joint grout
Small tube silicone sealant

*If you have a ready-made frame
you'll also need:*
sandpaper
cardboard
masking tape

BASIC TECHNIQUES
(see pages 20–23)

ALTERNATIVE DESIGNS
(see pages 60–61)

The black-and-white template for this project is on page 78.

1 Seal the frame with sealer to make it waterproof and leave it to dry for 60 minutes. If the frame is varnished or painted then sand the surface; if you are using a frame with a mirror

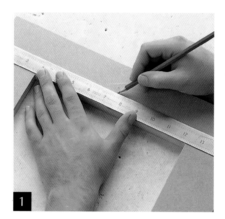

already in place then use cardboard and masking tape to cover and protect it. Measure the halfway point of each side of the frame and draw a horizontal line across so that you are left with four quarters to work on, one at a time.

2 Cut an equal amount of each color into halves for the inside edge and quarters for the inner border of the frame: cut around 12 of each color to get the half pieces (about 50), and 9 of each to get the quarter pieces (about 35). To do this, position the nippers at the middle edge of the tessera and nip – the tessera should snap into two halves. To get quarters, nip half tesserae in half again. Starting in one corner, lay the tesserae in place to make sure the pattern fits the frame. If it doesn't,

4 Grout, clean, and polish (see Steps 5 and 6, page 21). Turn the frame over and stick the mirror face-downward onto the back with silicone sealant. To do this accurately, position the mirror in place on the back of the frame and draw around it with a pencil. Remove the mirror, then apply a thin bead of sealant between your drawn line and the edge of the frame. Reposition the mirror and secure in place with masking tape.

you can adjust the amount of space (or grouting) between tesserae. You could, of course, adapt the design if you wish, adding or taking away a row or two of tesserae. Once you are happy with the layout you can start gluing.

3 Using the scraper, cover a quarter of the frame with the tile adhesive. Start sticking the tesserae into place, working from the outer edge inward to where the quarter-size tesserae form the inner border. Once you have completed one quarter, repeat the process until the whole frame is covered. Apply tile adhesive on the outside edge of the frame and cover with whole-size tesserae all the way around, lining up the colors with those on the face. Then place the half-size tesserae around the inside edge. You could use half-size tesserae for the outer edge as an alternative. Leave for about 24 hours until dry.

Classical-style lampbase

THE DESIGN FOR THIS LAMPBASE IS BOTH ELEGANT and simple, and the project is one of the easiest and quickest to make in the book. Its elegance lies in the use of only one color and of the single repeated Roman-inspired fan motif. The subtle coloring means that the design relies on the motif itself and the pattern of the grouting or interstices to add interest and movement. This project is a good example of the role grouting plays in simplifying and stylizing mosaic design for maximum impact. The pale cream color also means that this mosaic would fit in most interiors, but if you would prefer a colorful lampbase, then the one featured on the jacket may inspire you; it uses exactly the same design as this one, but in graduated shades of turquoise. The terracotta lampbase shape is a standard one, and is readily available from lighting stores. But don't worry if you can't get this exact lampbase, since it is easy to adapt the pattern to another shape. For safety reasons, make sure that no water gets into the hole for the electrical cord.

YOU WILL NEED

Basic Equipment (see page 20)

Tools
Water-soluble pen
Glass cutter
Tile cutter and breaker (see page 19)
Small pointing trowel

Materials
Lampbase about 11 inches high
1 quart ready-mixed tile adhesive
Ceramic tiles 6 inches x 6 inches:
  8 x satin cream
3-pound bag of ivory wide-
  joint grout

BASIC TECHNIQUES
(see pages 20–23)

ALTERNATIVE DESIGNS
(see pages 62–63)

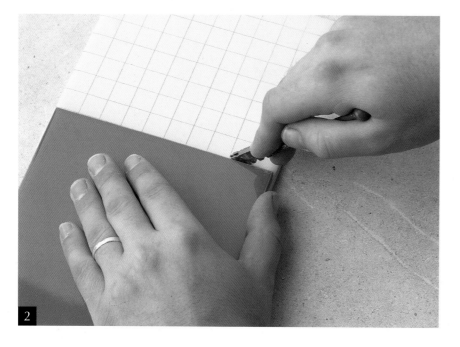

The black-and-white template for this project is on page 79.

1 In pencil, divide the lampbase, from top to bottom, into 5 equal bands to act as guidelines. Turn the lampbase on its side and pencil in four equal points around the circumference of the base. At each point draw an arc, or half a fan, and then continue upward, drawing in fan shapes.

2 Using a ruler and water-soluble pen, mark up approximately 8 tiles into ⅝-inch squares. Use a glass cutter to score along the drawn lines, pressing it against the edge of another tile.

3 Cut along the scored lines using the tile cutter and breaker, first into strips and then into squares (see page 23). To do this, position the tile in the teeth of the breaker, aligning the pointer with the scored line and pushing it up as far as it will go, then grasp the handles together firmly to cut the tile cleanly.

4 Using the small pointing trowel, apply adhesive to one marked fan shape at a time, and stick down the tesserae in rows, working from the outer curve inward. The final tessera in each fan shape will need to be cut into a triangle to fit the V-shaped tip (see page 20). Leave to dry for 24 hours, then grout, clean, and polish (see Steps 5 and 6, page 21).

3

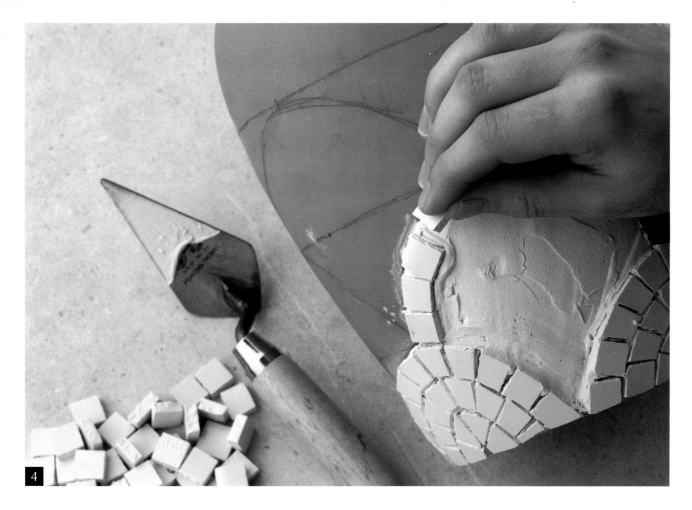

4

Kitsch kitchen vase

ANOTHER QUICK AND EASY PROJECT AND PROBABLY the most fun and colorful, inspired by the gaudy flower prints of the late Sixties and early Seventies. It is made up of ceramic tiles, cut into small tesserae and combined with glass beads, so it's a great way to use up old or reject tiles. Patterned tiles or smashed china could also be used, but give some thought to how the patterns and colors work together so that contrast and definition aren't lost. To heighten color, a bright green grout is used — colored grouts can either be bought ready-made, or made by adding acrylic paint to a neutral-colored grout. Bright grouting is a good way of enlivening mosaic pieces. When working with a 3-D form such as this, it is important to keep the tesserae small so that they don't protrude and the surface is kept as smooth as possible. You could use any shape or size of vase (though the instructions on the following pages obviously relate to the one shown) and any other 3-D object — such as a lampbase, sculpture, or statue.

YOU WILL NEED

Basic Equipment (see page 20)

Tools
Tile cutter and breaker (see page 19)

Materials
Vase, about 9½ inches high
1 quart ready-mixed water-resistant
  tile adhesive
Ceramic tiles 6 inches x 6 inches:
  3 x shades of green
  2 x yellow
  2 x orange
  2 x white
10 colored glass beads
3-pound bag of white wide-
  joint grout, plus green acrylic
  paint or 3-pound bag green grout

BASIC TECHNIQUES
(see pages 20–23)

ALTERNATIVE DESIGNS
(see pages 64–65)

The black-and-white template for this project is on page 80.

1 Cut the tiles into strips; some ½-inch and some ¾-inch wide (see Steps 1 and 2, page 23), then nip these into rough wedge shapes or triangles, to give a variety of petal sizes. Nip the green tiles into small irregularly shaped pieces, no larger than ½-inch square. These will be used to fill in the spaces between the flowers.

2 Glass beads are used for some of the flower centers, but to add variety of texture and size, cut up a few tile pieces into circular shapes. To do this, hold a ½-inch-square piece of tile in one hand and nip at the corners with the nippers in the other hand, turning as you do so, until you get a roughly circular shape.

3 Paste up a roughly tile-sized area of the vase at a time. Stick down a flower center, then arrange the wedge-shaped petals around it. If the petal pieces are too long, they will jut out and form sharp, protruding edges. Nip your petals down a little if this is the case. For our vase, we stuck down about 3 flowers at a time, overlapping a few so that some flowers appear to be hidden behind others.

4 Fill the areas between the flowers with green pieces. Repeat the process until the entire surface of the vase is covered. Clean off any excess adhesive with a damp sponge and leave to dry for 24 hours before grouting. The green grout used here can either be bought, or made up by mixing acrylic paint with white grout, but be careful not to stain your clothes or furniture. Grout, clean, and polish (see Steps 5 and 6, page 21).

Silver star picture frame

THE COMBINATION OF SILVER LEAF WITH WHITE porcelain tesserae in a simple design creates a stylish, contemporary look. This is not the least expensive project – silver tesserae are costly as they are made with silver leaf – but expense is kept down because only small amounts are needed here. The silver makes all the difference, as it catches the light and contrasts with the opaque porcelain. You could use gold if you prefer, although this is also expensive; if keeping costs down to a minimum is a priority, then try pieces of mirror glass instead of silver. To make the frame you (or your local carpenter or lumber supplier) will need to do the following: cut a 1-foot square out of ¾-inch fiberboard, and then cut a circle 7 inches in diameter from the center. Out of the back, cut an 8-inch square around the circle for the glass and picture to sit in. Alternatively, you could mosaic an existing frame, in which case you would need to sand it down and seal it with sealant. The direct method is used here but the indirect would also be possible.

YOU WILL NEED

Basic Equipment (see page 20)

Tools
Compass
Water-soluble pen
Glass cutter
Tile cutter and breaker (see page 19)

Materials
Picture frame 1 foot x 1 foot square
Sealant (1 part household glue to 4
  parts water)
1 quart ready-mixed
  water-resistant tile adhesive
80 x silver-leaf mosaic tesserae,
  ¾ inch x ¾ inch
150 x white porcelain tesserae
  1 inch x 1 inch
3-pound bag white wide-joint grout

BASIC TECHNIQUES
(see pages 20–23)

ALTERNATIVE DESIGNS
(see pages 66–67)

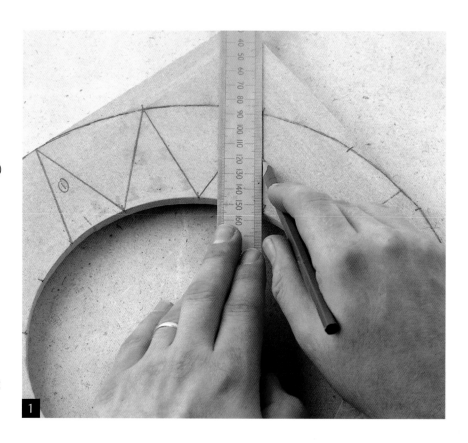

down in a circular pattern, starting at the outer edge and working inward. You'll need to nip them into smaller, triangular pieces as you get to the bottom of each V-shape. To fill the remaining four corners, paste up one at a time, and stick down the tesserae, again following the circular pattern. As in Step 2, lay each tessera over the edge of the picture frame, score, and cut. Make sure the tesserae do not overhang the frame edge.

4 To tile the inner and outer edges in white, you'll need to measure the thickness of your frame. For this frame, the half tesserae are the right size for the outer edge. For the inside edge, hold the tesserae upright against the edge, mark the necessary thickness in pencil, and then score and cut along the line. In order to make sure that the tesserae do not hang below where the glass will go, turn the frame over and press down with a tile to make sure that everything is level. Cut all the pieces you need (about 20) into halves, and then apply adhesive to each edge before sticking down. Once complete, clean the mosaic with a damp sponge and leave to dry for 24 hours. Then grout, clean, and polish (see Steps 5 and 6, page 21), and replace the glass in the frame.

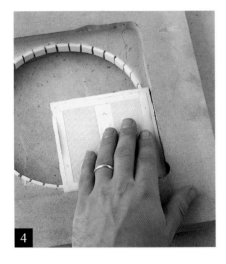

The black-and-white template for this project is on page 81.

1 Remove the glass from your frame and put it in a safe place. Seal the frame with sealant and leave to dry. Using the compass, draw a circle that fills the frame so that it touches the outer edge at each side. Mark 16 points around this circle at slightly different intervals so that the spikes vary in size. Draw in the spikes from these points to 16 points marked on the inner edge, using the template as a guide if necessary.

2 If you are using the same frame size as ours you will find that each spike uses about 3 silver-leaf tesserae in length. To cut the tesserae so that they fit the spike shape, lay them on the spike and mark with the water-soluble pen where the lines of the spike run under the tile. Score with the glass cutter, break with the tile cutter and breaker, and then stick the tesserae down, one spike at a time.

3 Cut the porcelain tesserae into quarters using the nippers, and don't worry if they are slightly irregular. Apply adhesive to each inverse spike and stick the tesserae

Mediterranean-style dish

SMALL SQUARE TESSERAE ARE CAREFULLY GRADUATED to create an aquamarine sea background for these gold-colored fish – these are made up of irregularly shaped pieces so that each one looks different. The entire mosaic is created using vitreous glass tesserae, which are not only particularly suitable for color fades, but are also thin enough not to add too much weight or bulk to the dish. This is an easy design to follow but it will still take up to a day in total to complete, because the adhesive needs to be left to dry overnight. This is always the case when glass material is applied to a glazed surface and means that you need to take special care when cleaning off excess adhesive from the tesserae before they are completely set, to avoid dislodging them. The original dish was highly patterned, as you can see in the step-by-step photographs overleaf, and in fact was sold as a reject – a reminder that mosaic can give a new lease on life to objects that are faulty or ugly! As this is a 3-D project, the direct method is used.

YOU WILL NEED

Basic Equipment (see page 20)

Tools
Permanent marker
Scissors

Materials
Platter dish 15 inches in diameter
Stiff paper or cardboard
1 quart ready-mix tile adhesive
Vitreous glass tesserae (Vetricolor):
  85 x very light aqua (20.35.2)
  65 x light aqua (20.42.2)
  55 x aqua (20.57.2)
  45 x dark aqua (20.67.2)
  30 x dark orange (20.99.3)
  30 x light orange (20.79.3)
3-pound bag gray wide-
  joint grout

BASIC TECHNIQUES
(see pages 20–23)

ALTERNATIVE DESIGNS
(see pages 68–69)

The black-and-white template for this project is on page 82.

1 Using a permanent marker, draw 8 lines from the center of the bowl outward to give you 8 equal segments. Mark 3 equal points along each line and then join up to create 4 concentric circles. These will be your guidelines for positioning the tesserae.

2 Draw and cut out a simple fish motif from stiff paper or cardboard, about the size of the one shown here. On each of the 8 lines, and on the outermost guideline, draw around the motif to end up with 8 fish, each pointing in the same direction.

3 Nip the two shades of orange tesserae into small, irregular pieces, then paste up and fill in the fish shapes, keeping to the drawn outlines, one at a time. Nip some of the tesserae into triangular-shaped pieces in order to form the head and tail.

4 To fill in the blue background, start with about 5 rows of the darkest color in the center. Then work outward, gradually fading from dark to light. Graduate as follows: for every 3 tesserae of the darker shade on one row, add one of the lighter; then, on the next row, for every 3 of the lighter shade, add one of the darker. Then create 2–3 solid lines of the lighter shade, and so on, until the entire surface is covered. When you reach the fish motifs, you will have to nip the tesserae into triangular or wedge-shaped pieces to fit round them. Clean off excess adhesive with a damp sponge before leaving to dry for 24 hours. Finally, grout, clean, and polish (see Steps 5 and 6, page 21).

African-style tabletop

PRIMITIVE AFRICAN TRIBAL PAINTINGS INSPIRED THIS bold, simple design and vibrant color scheme. This is not a difficult design, but the project will take up to two days to complete because of the length of time needed for the glue to dry. Ceramic tiles are widely available everywhere but most of those used here were picked up in close-out stores or at yard sales. These are excellent places for the bargain-hunter – even the ugliest tiles have potential, as the gaudy orange tiles used here prove. Charcoal grout unifies the piece and adds to its impact, but take care as it stains easily when wet. The top, with a diameter of 2 feet, was cut from 1-inch fiberboard but a local carpenter or lumber supplier could easily do this for you. The base was made by a local iron forger but ready-made bases are also widely available. Alternatively, of course, you could mosaic an existing table. For a project like this, in which the tiles are of different thicknesses, it is easier to use the indirect method which allows you to get the flat surface needed for a tabletop.

YOU WILL NEED

Basic Equipment (see page 20)

Tools
Craft knife
1-inch artist's brush
Scissors
Kitchen towel
Hammer
Glass cutter
Tile cutter and breaker (see page 19)
Combed scraper or spatula
Block of wood

Materials
Tabletop 2 feet in diameter,
  cut from 1-inch-thick fiberboard
Sealant (1 part household glue to
  4 parts water)
Brown paper
Washable household glue
Ceramic tiles 6 inches x 6 inches:
  6 x mottled brown
  3 x plain orange
  3 x mottled orange
  13 x black
  2 x bronze
1 quart ready-mixed water-resistant
  tile adhesive
3-pound bag of charcoal wide-joint
  grout

BASIC TECHNIQUES
(see pages 20–23)

ALTERNATIVE DESIGNS
(see pages 70–71)

The black-and-white template for this project is on page 83.

1 Using the craft knife, score the entire surface of the tabletop and then seal with sealant, using the artist's brush. Leave to dry. Cut out a piece of brown paper the exact size of the tabletop. Reserve about 1 bronze tile and 5 black tiles to be used for the table edge. To get the irregular black and orange pieces you need for the surface, bundle the tiles up, one at a time, into a kitchen towel and smash lightly with a hammer. Go easy on this; you want to end up with large and small coin-sized pieces, not smithereens! Remember to keep the different colors in three separate piles, to avoid confusion.

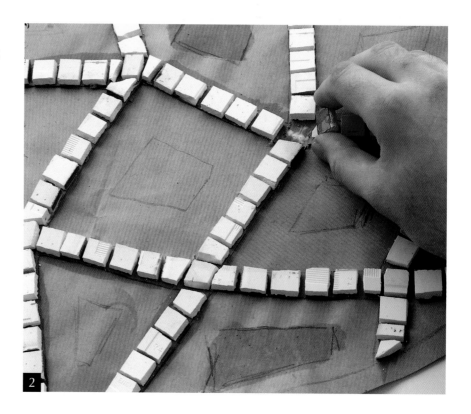

2 Draw approximately 25 irregular diamond shapes, about 4 inches square, over the paper, with smaller, similar shapes in the center of each. Using the tile cutter and breaker, cut the brown and bronze tiles into ⅝-inch strips, then cut about 4 of the bronze strips and all of the brown strips into ½-inch squares (see page 23). Using washable household glue, stick the brown tesserae face downward, then position the bronze tesserae to fit the space where the lines intersect. Note that all the tesserae will appear white since they are upside-down, but if you stick them down in the right order – first the brown tesserae, then the bronze – you won't get confused.

3 Apply glue to each irregular square. First stick down the orange tesserae, mixing the two shades, then fill in the surrounding area with black.

4 Once the mosaic has dried on, you can transfer it to the tabletop. Using a combed scraper or spatula, paste up the surface of the tabletop, then turn upside-down and place on top of the mosaic. Push down firmly, using the block of wood. When dry, (after about 24 hours) turn over, dampen the brown paper, and peel it off. Remove any excess glue by rubbing with a wet cloth, using the craft knife to gouge out any stubborn areas if necessary. Next, cut the remaining black and bronze tiles into strips to the thickness of the edge. Stick down all around the edge, lining up the bronze strips with the bronze tesserae on the surface. Some of the tops of these strips will be white, but the charcoal grout will stain them black. Leave to dry for 24 hours then grout, clean, and polish (see Steps 5 and 6, page 21).

3

4

Pebble urn for outdoors

THIS PROJECT, WITH ITS CLASSIC PEBBLE DECORATION, was especially designed for the garden, and so a large, frostproof terracotta urn and exterior-quality powder-mix adhesive were used. The limited use of smalti for the zigzag motif, combined with porcelain tesserae and pebbles, keeps the cost of this project down. The pebbles are, of course, free and can be collected from beaches, parks, or gardens – choose small, smooth ones, and aim for a mixture of gray and white to match the colors of the mosaic. The design is simple and easy to follow but it will take time to cover the large surface area, and it is worth taking care when drawing the zigzag motif, ensuring it joins up well. To achieve a finished look, clean as you go along, taking care not to snag the smalti or pebbles. Leave it to dry totally, then wash and scrub using a scouring brush and a phosphoric acid-based cleaner before rinsing with clean water. The white-painted rim tones in well, but you could stick with the terracotta or try a rich color, such as blue or green, for a brighter look.

YOU WILL NEED

Basic Equipment (see page 20)

Tools
1-inch artist's brush
Scissors

Materials
Terracotta urn 12 inches high
  (frostproof if for outdoor use)
Sealant (1 part household glue to
  4 parts water)
Stiff paper or cardboard
I quart adhesive
  (or 11-pound bag of exterior-
  quality powder-mix adhesive
  if urn is for outdoor use)
White eggshell latex paint
Small pebbles
Smalti:
  50 x dark blue (69)
  50 x light blue (70)
Porcelain tesserae (1 inch x 1 inch):
  150 x gray-blue (112)
3-pound bag white
  wide-joint grout

BASIC TECHNIQUES
(see pages 20–23)

ALTERNATIVE DESIGNS
(see pages 72–73)

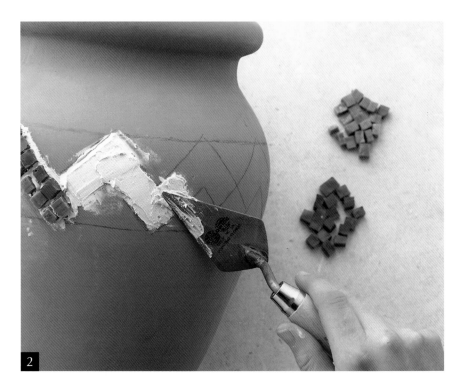

The black-and-white template for this project is on page 84.

1 Seal the urn with sealant, using the artist's brush. To make a V-shaped template for the zigzag, first cut all the blue smalti into halves. Lay them out in an arrowhead shape on stiff paper or card, then draw around the shape and cut it out. Draw a line on the urn where the bottom of the zigzag will be, and a second, parallel line 3 inches above it, to create a strip in which to draw the zigzag.

2 Align the template with the marked lines on the urn, and draw around it to mark a zigzag all around the urn.

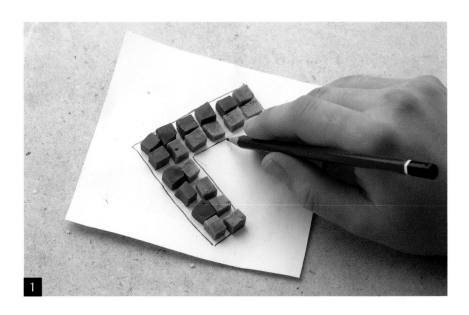

Paste up the zigzag area, and stick down the tesserae in sections so that the adhesive does not dry out.

3 Cut the gray porcelain tesserae into quarters. Starting at the bottom of the urn, apply adhesive and stick down the tesserae in bands, again to prevent the adhesive from drying out. Continue in this way until you reach the zigzag where you will have to cut the quarters into triangles to fit (see page 20). Clean off any excess adhesive as you go along, being careful not to move the tesserae.

If you wait until you have completely finished sticking them down before you do this, the adhesive may dry hard and will be difficult to remove.

4 Paint the rim of the pot in white eggshell paint and leave to dry before you mosaic above the zigzag line. You could, of course, choose another color for the rim – gray or pale blue would be obvious alternatives for matching the color scheme. Paste up small areas at a time, using generous amounts of adhesive, and then stick down the pebbles, spacing them out roughly as shown. Once you have finished, clean the surface of the pebbles as in Step 3. Leave the mosaic to dry for 24 hours. Grout, clean, and polish (see Steps 5 and 6, page 21).

Half-moon tabletop

THIS ELEGANT CONSOLE TABLETOP, WITH ITS SUBDUED color scheme and subtle border patterns, should suit a range of interiors and tastes. It has perhaps the most intricate design of all our projects and so complete beginners may not want to start off with this one. The indirect method is recommended for this project because it enables you to follow the drawn design more easily (see page 22). The tabletop needs to be cut (either by yourself, a local carpenter, or lumber supplier) from 1-inch fiberboard as follows: cut a semicircle with an 18-inch diameter; measure 2½ inches in from the straight edge; draw a parallel line and cut along it. You should now have the truncated semicircular shape needed for this project. The chic aluminum legs came from a company that specializes in aluminum casting, but you could buy a ready-made base or have one made by a metalworker. The project will take up to two days to complete because of the length of time needed for the glue to dry before you can transfer the mosaic to the tabletop.

YOU WILL NEED

Basic Equipment (see page 20)

Tools

Craft knife
1-inch artist's brush
Scissors
Water-soluble pen
Glass cutter
Tile cutter and breaker (see page 19)
Combed scraper or spatula
Squeegee or block of wood

Materials

Tabletop, 3-feet long at straight
  edge, cut from 1-inch
  thick fiberboard
Sealant (1 part household glue to
  4 parts water)
Brown paper
Washable household glue
Vitreous glass tesserae (Vetricolor):
  200 x white gold vein (Le Gemme
    20.20.4)
  80 x Russet Gold Blend
  55 x gold (20.10.4)
Porcelain tesserae (1 inch x 1 inch)
  200 x old rose
  100 x beige
1 quart pot ready-mixed water-
  resistant tile adhesive
3-pound bag ivory wide-
  joint grout

BASIC TECHNIQUES

(see pages 20–23)

ALTERNATIVE DESIGNS

(see pages 74–75)

The black-and-white template for this project is on page 85.

1 Using the craft knife, score the fiberboard tabletop and seal with sealant, including the edges and underside, using the artist's brush. Leave until completely dry, about 1 hour. Lay the tabletop on a sheet of brown paper, draw around it, and cut out. Use a porcelain tessera to gauge the width of the outer border and draw a line all around.

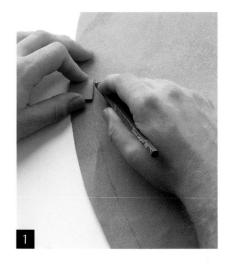

2 From the line you have drawn, draw the remaining 3 guidelines. To do this, measure in about 3½ glass tesserae, 4 porcelain tesserae, and then 3½ glass tesserae. Now draw in the 2 wavy lines as shown below, using the template as a guide if necessary. Using the artist's brush, apply washable household glue to the outer edge of the brown paper. Stick down the outside ring of porcelain tiles face downward, mixing the two shades. When this is done, leave a ¹⁄₁₆-inch grout gap before starting the next border. Remember to leave a gap between each row of tesserae.

3 Starting with the wavy line, paste and stick down a continuous line of white tesserae, smooth side downward. Beneath and above the wavy line, you will have a series of semicircular shapes which you should mosaic one at a time. Follow the template, working outward from the

wavy line. First stick down half-tesserae of the Russet Gold Blend, then more white, and finally the gold tesserae (see Step 4), always allowing a ⅟₁₆-inch grout gap. You may need to cut some tesserae into wedge shapes to make them fit (see page 20).

4 When you come to the edge of the tabletop and are filling in the gold-colored tesserae, hold them over the edge, mark where they need cutting using the water-soluble pen, and score with a glass cutter or tile cutter and breaker and break using the latter. Continue in this way until the border is finished. Repeat the whole process for the inner border.

To complete the project:

To fill in the remaining areas with a mix of the two shades of porcelain tesserae, first count and reserve the amount needed for the table edge (about 50) and for the center border (about 150). Quarter the remainder. Paste up the center and stick down the quarters in straight lines. Finally paste up and fill in the area between the wavy borders with full-size pieces laid out in a circular pattern. Leave to dry for 24 hours. Using a combed spatula or scraper, paste the table surface with water-resistant adhesive, then turn upside down and place on top of the mosaic, making sure the curved edge aligns. Press down firmly with a squeegee or block of wood. Paste up the table edge and stick down the whole porcelain tiles, mixing the two shades. Leave to dry for 24 hours. Soak the brown paper with a damp sponge and peel off in one piece. Clean off any excess adhesive with a wet cloth. Finally grout, clean, and polish (see steps 5 and 6, page 21).

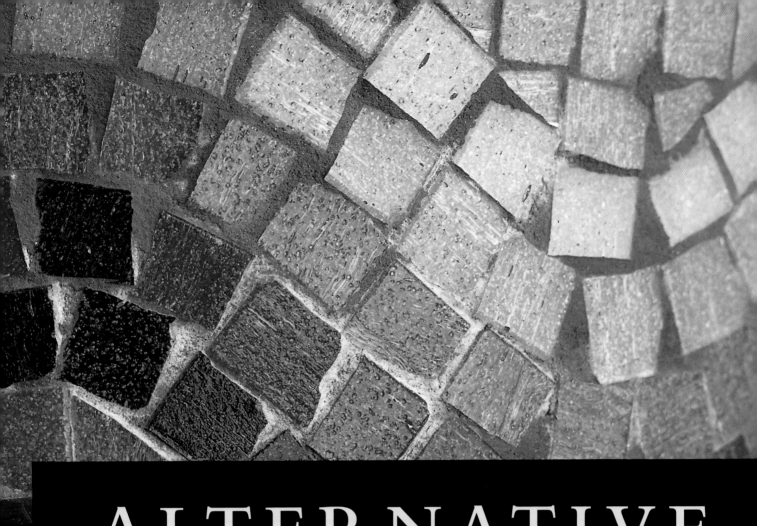

ALTERNATIVE DESIGNS

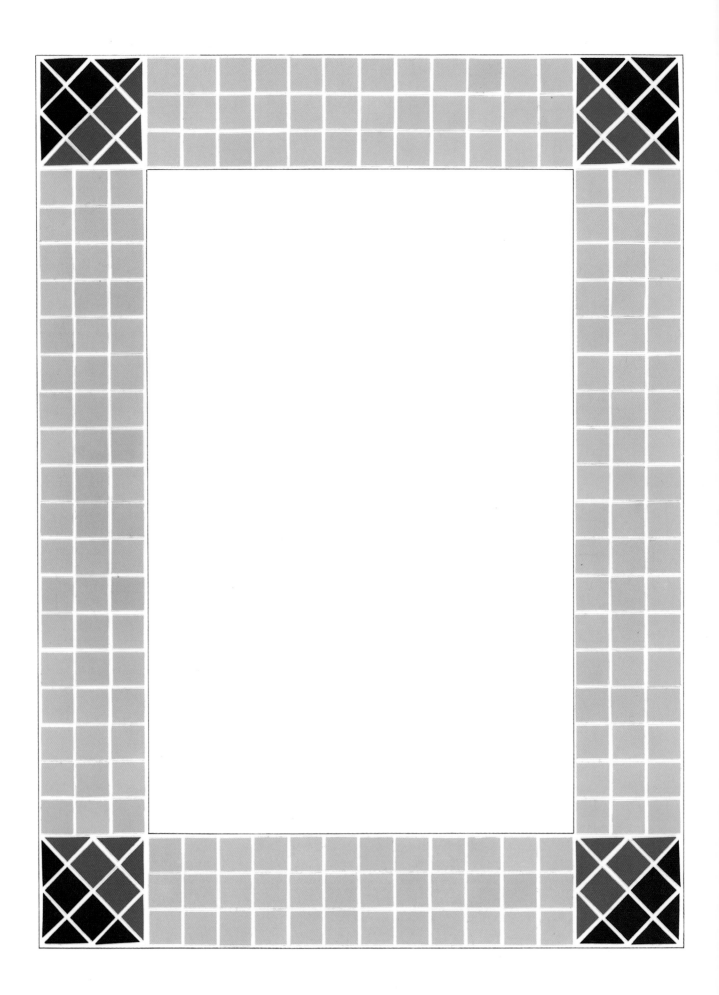

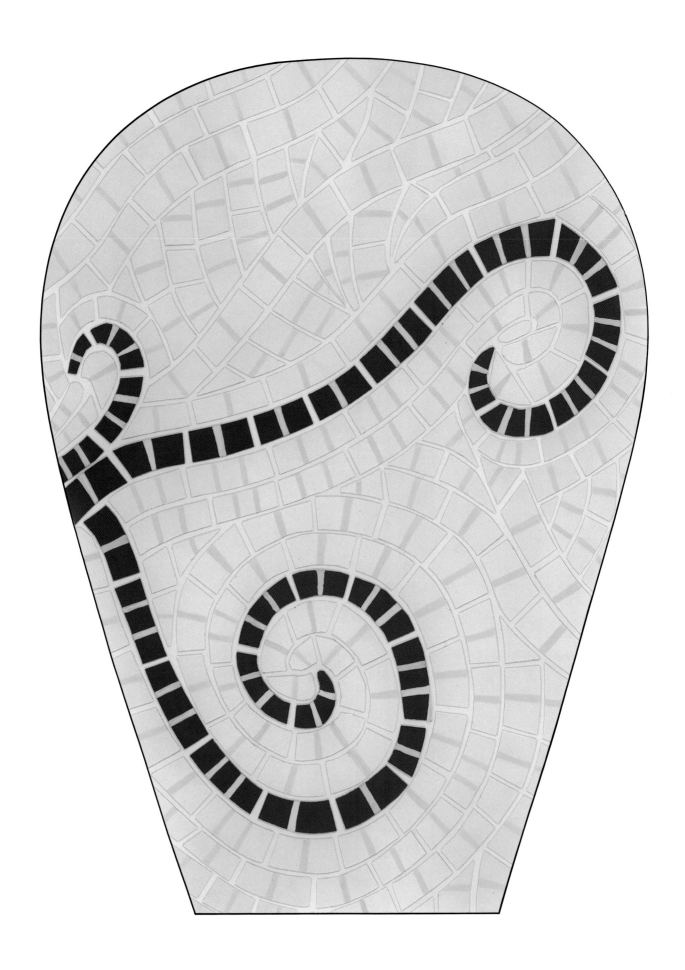

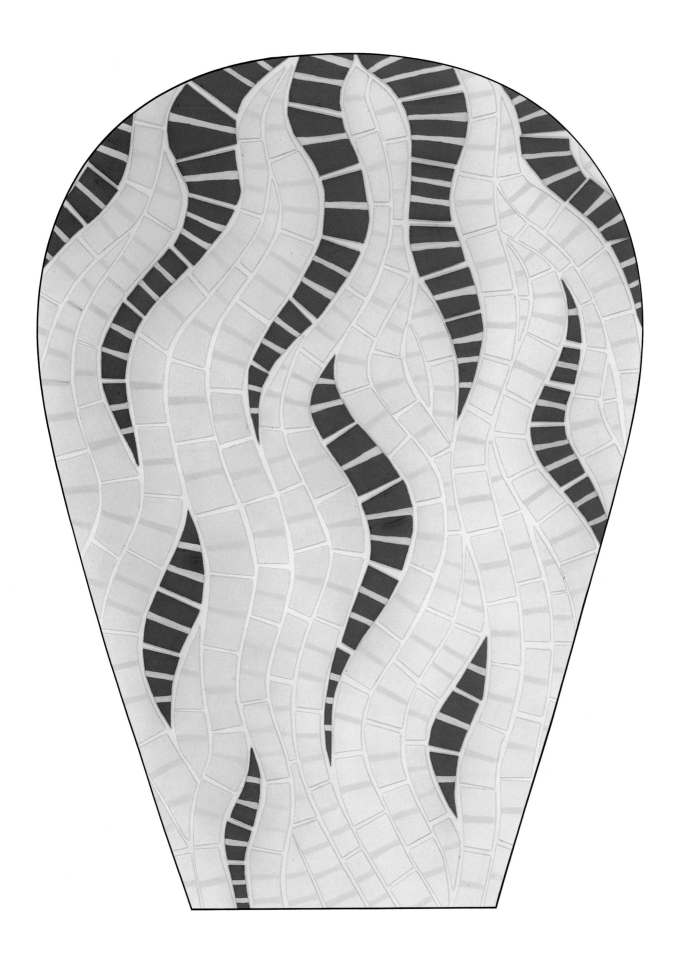

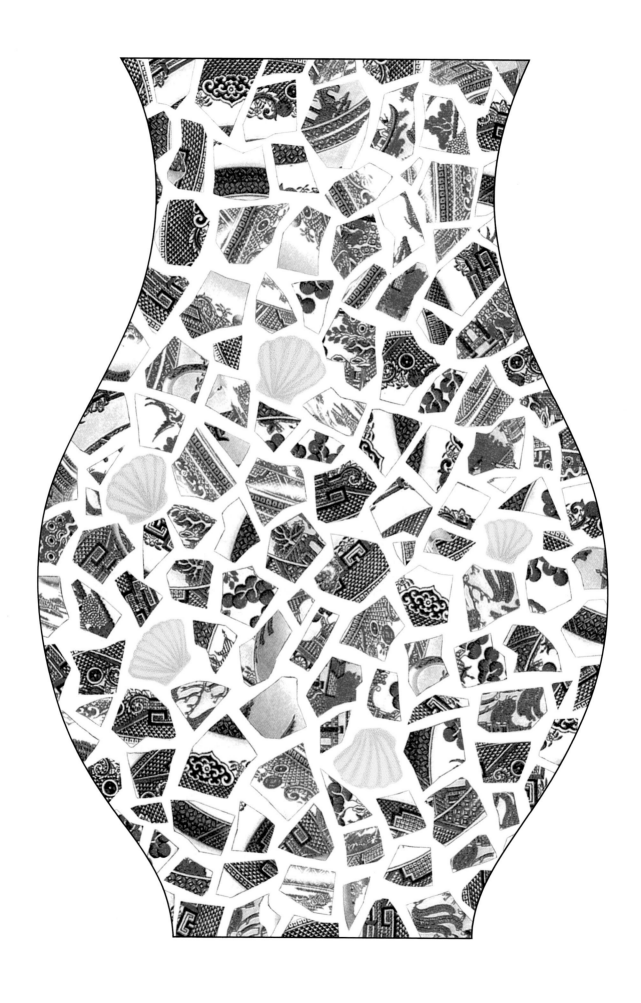

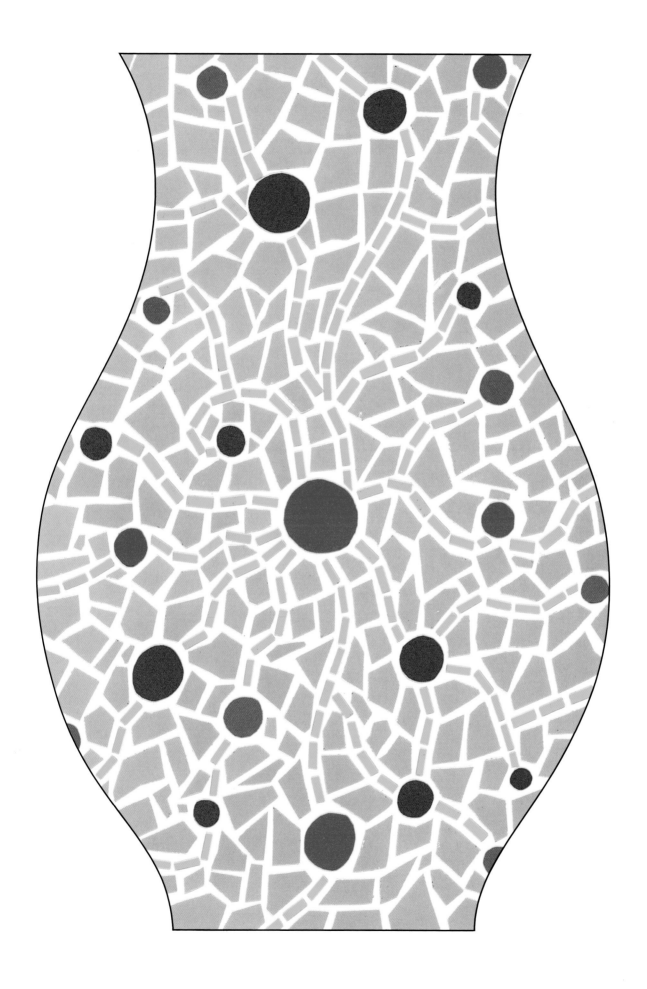

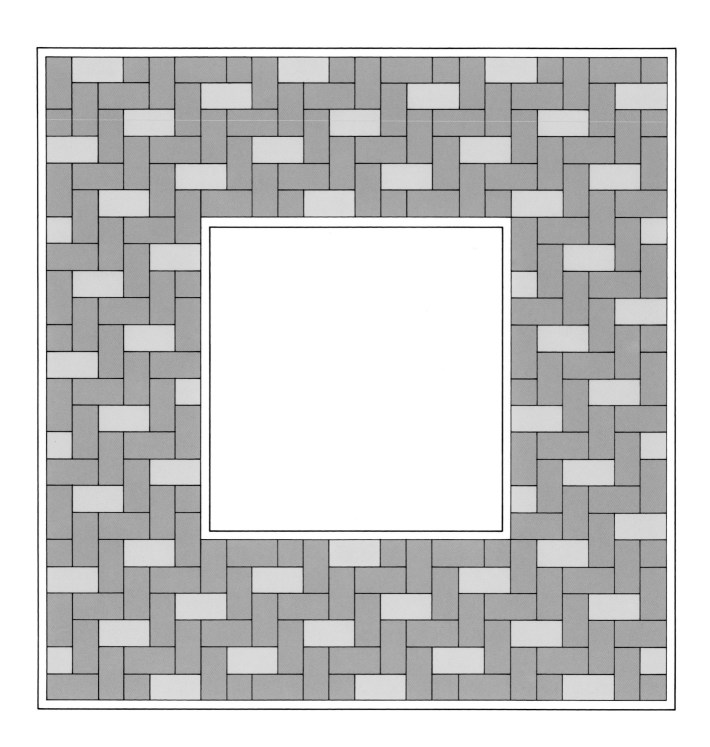

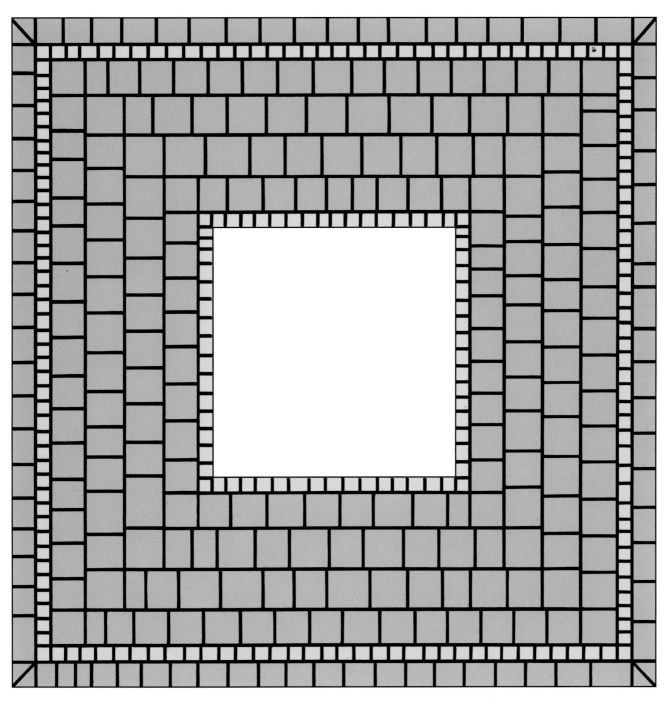

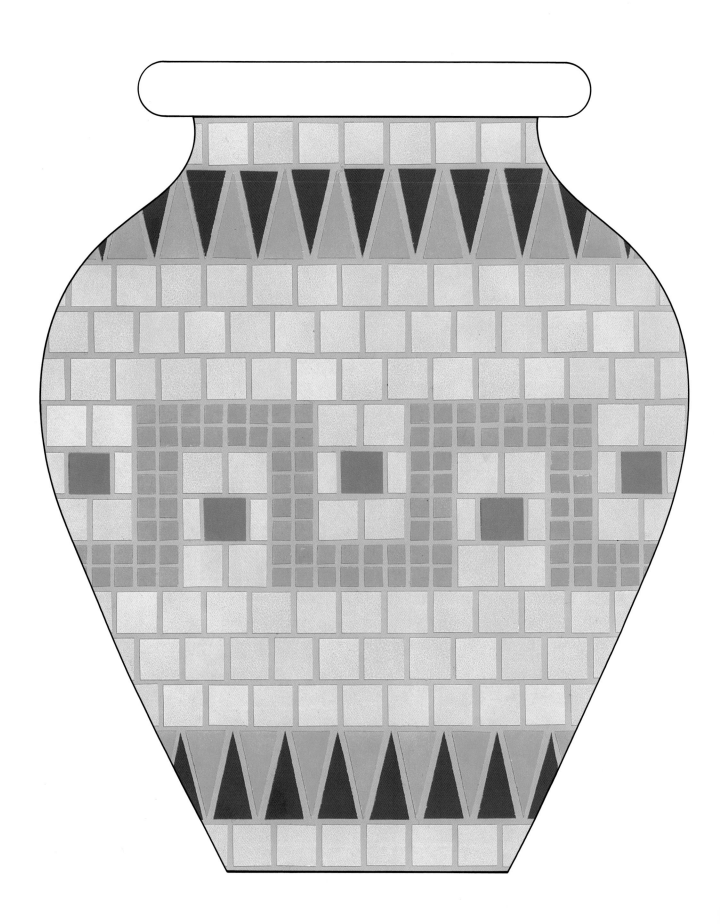

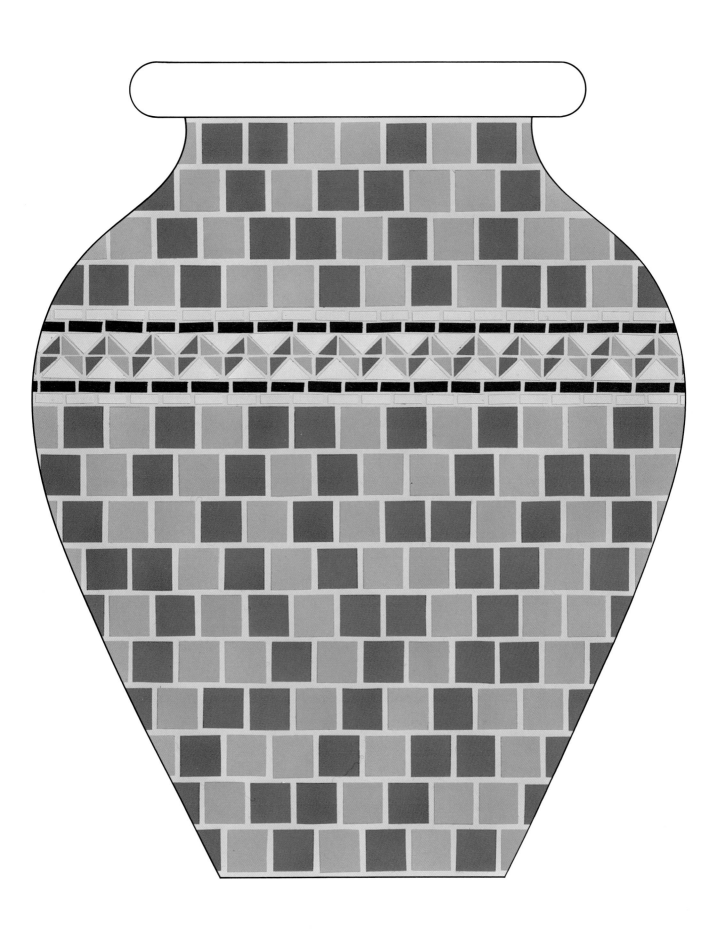

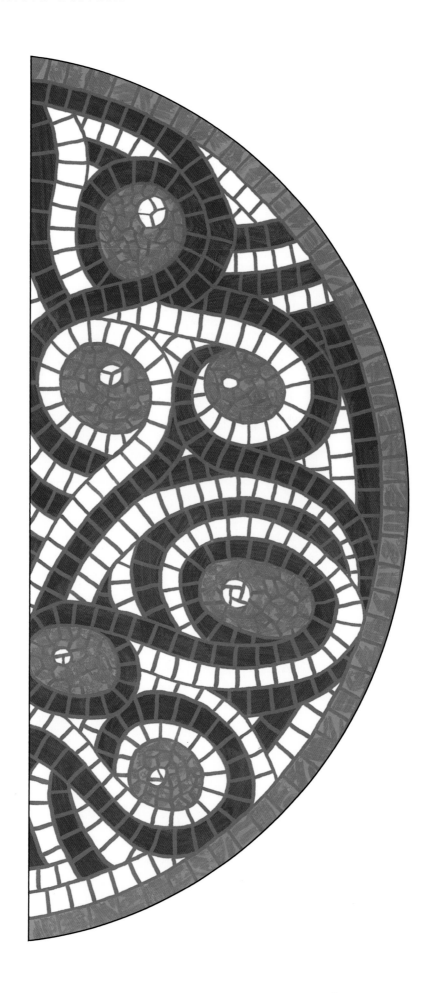

TEMPLATES
& MOTIFS

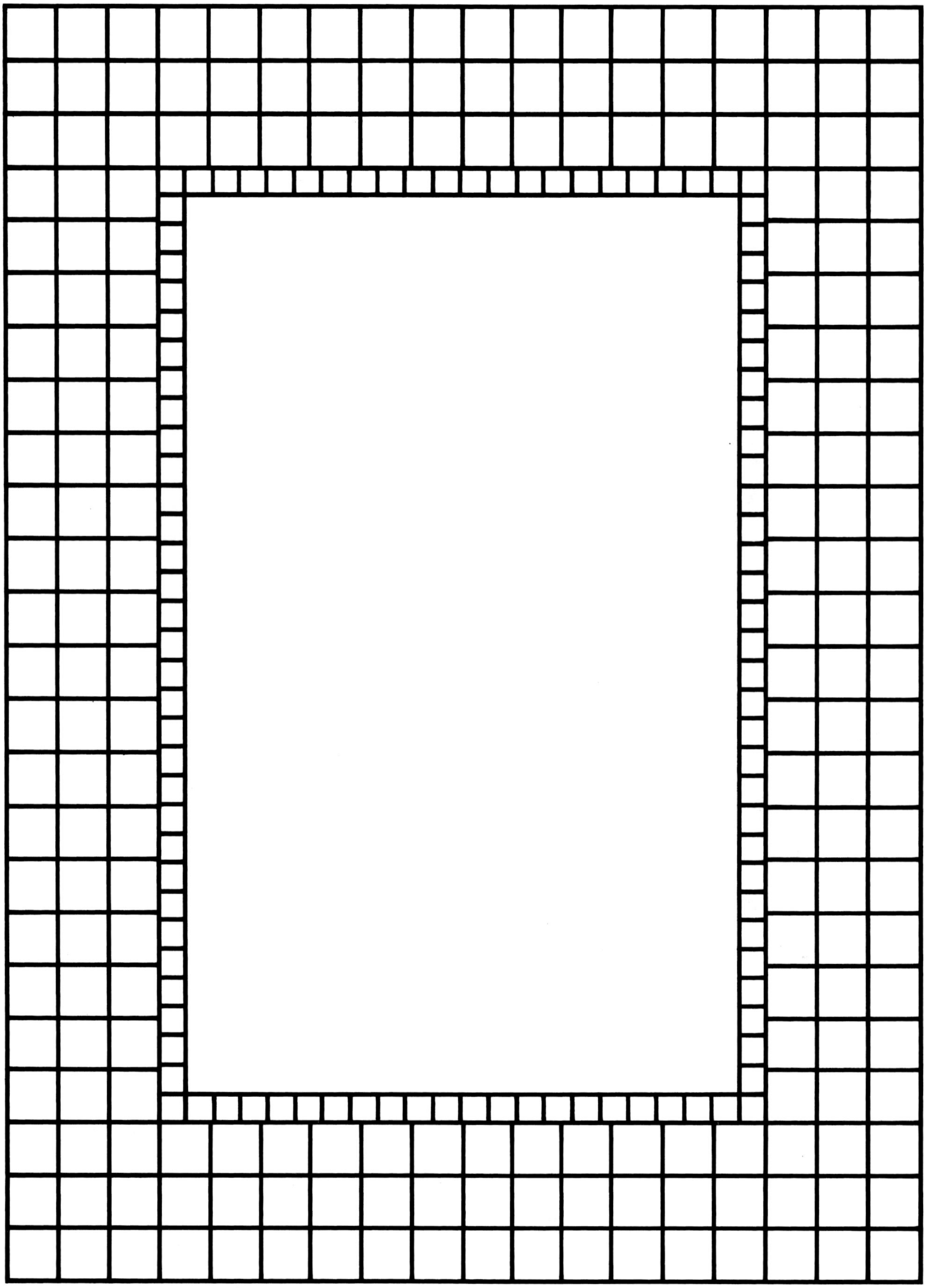

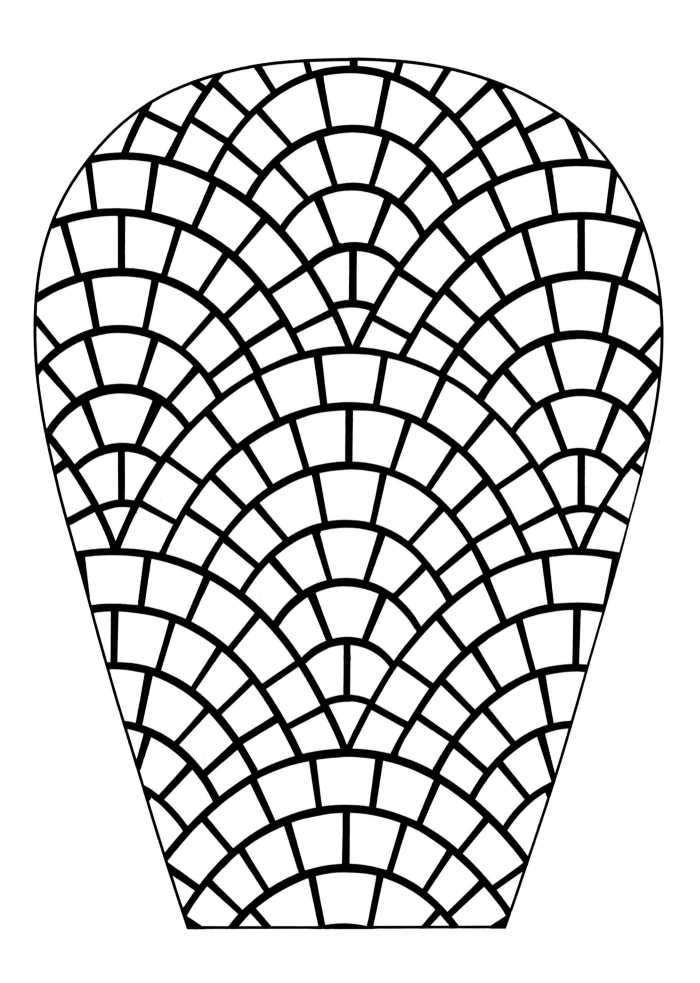

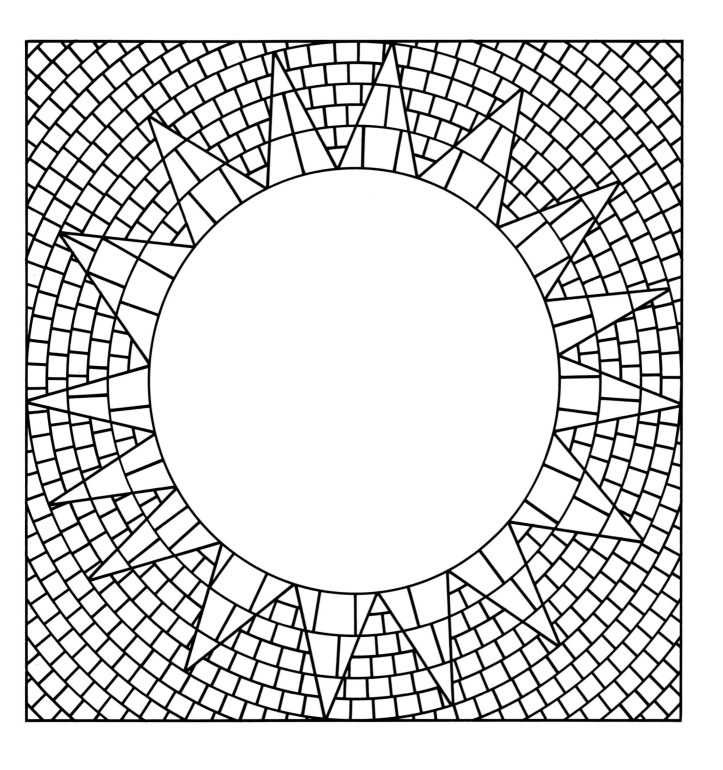

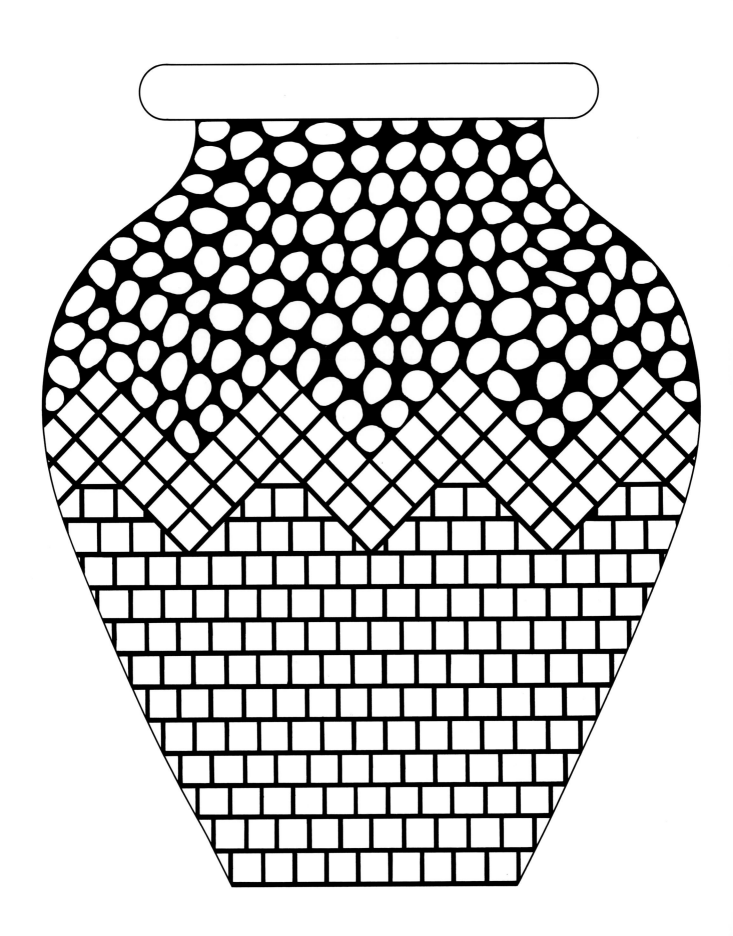

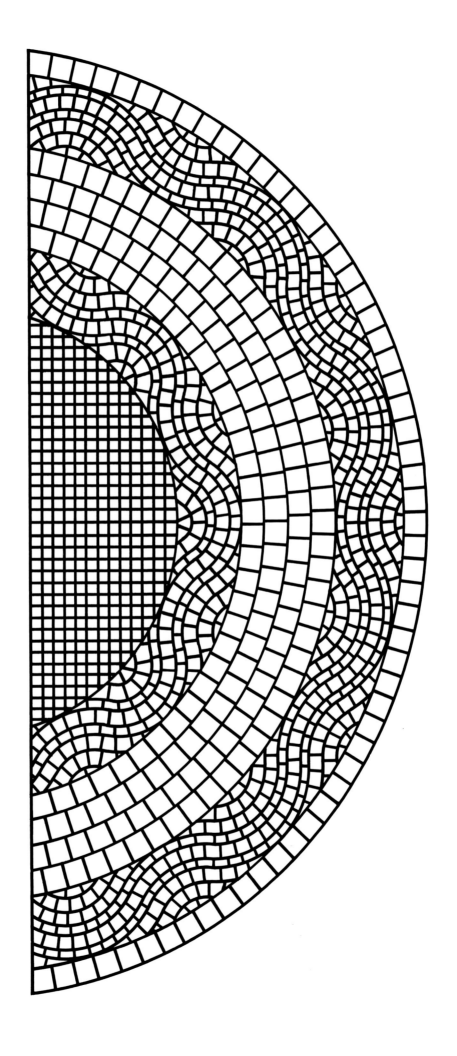

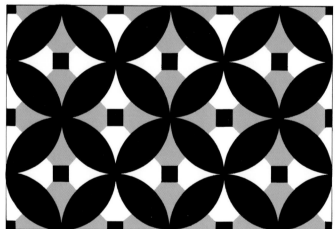

American Craft Council
American Craft Enterprises
21 South Eltings Corner Road
Highland, NY 12528
Tel: 800 836 3470

Arizona Art Supply
3236 N. 3rd Street
Phoenix, AZ 85012
Tel: 602 264 9514

Champion's Craft and Decorating, Inc
9750 Regency Square Blvd.
Jacksonville, FL 32225
Tel: 904 725 3020

Crafter's Market of Minnesota, Inc.
896 County Road 42 West
Burnsville, MN 55337
Tel: 612 898 4664

D&L Stained Glass
4939 North Broadway
Boulder, CO 80304
Tel: 303 449 8737

Delphi Stained Glass
2116 E. Michigan Ave.
Lansing, MI 48912
Tel: 517 482 2617

Dunn Toys and Hobbies, Inc.
166 South Beach St.
Daytona Beach, FL 32114
Tel: 904 253 3644

Ed Hoy's International
1620 Frontenac Road
Naperville, IL 60563
Tel: 708 420 0890

Glass Crafters
398 Interstate Court
Sarasota, FL 34240
Tel: 941 379 8333

Glass Emporium
322 Pennsylvania Ave.
North Wales, PA 19454
Tel: 215 699 7007

Kurfecs Coatings Inc.
201 East Market Street
Louisville, KY 40202

Michael's Craft and Floral Warehouse
304 Constitution Dr.
Virginia Beach, VA 23462
Tel: 804 552 0772

Mosaic Mercantile
215 East Lewis 303
PO Box 1550
Livingston, MT 59047
Tel: 406 222 0990

Plaid Enterprises Inc.
PO Box 7600
Norcross, GA 30091–7600

Priscilla's Publications and Products
8158 East 44th Street
PO Box 45730
Tulsa, OK 74145

Sven Warner-Mountaintop Mosaic
PO Box 653
Main Street
Castleton, VT 05735
Tel: 802 468 3019

Treasure House Stores, Inc.
5959 Corson Ave. South
Seattle, WA 98108
Tel: 206 762 1561

Authors' acknowledgments

Paul and Paul would like to thank everyone at Conran Octopus, Joe Joyce at The Studio and Christine Brickman at Wallis and all our families.